ORGAN BLUE BOSSA

Grimoaldo Macchia

H. T. FitzSimons Company
Exclusively Distributed by
Hal•Leonard

For my friend, Alessandro Albenga

Organ Blue Bossa

Grimoaldo Macchia

Sw. Flute 8', 4', Vox. Cel. 8', Echo Cel. 8', Octave 4'
Gt. Harm. Fl. 8', Rohrflute 8', Flute 4', Twelfth 2⅔', Sw. to Gt.
Ch. Bourdon 8', Salicional 8', Flute 4', Oboe 8' (Corno di Bassetto 8')
Ped. Principal 16, Subbass 16', Octave 8', Gedackt 8', Gt. to Ped.

10
13
16
19
1
Gt. -Twelfth 2⅔'
+Cornet 8' (Trumpet 8')
Sw. +Krummhorn 8' (Oboe 8')
2
Gt. -Cornet 8' (Trumpet 8')
+Twelfth 2⅔'
Sw. -Krummhorn 8' (Oboe 8')
+Octave 2'
Ped. +4'

22
25
27
1
Gt. -Twelfth 2⅔'
+Trumpet 8'
30
2
Slower blues feel ♩= 108
Gt. -Cornet 8' (Trumpet 8')
+Ch. to Gt.
rit.
(Blues improvisation)
Sw. +Tremulant
Ped. -4'

32
(Sw.)
35
38
Gt. +Cornet 8' (Trumpet 8')
Sw. +Krummhorn 8' (Oboe 8')
Ped. -Gt. to Ped.
Resume bossa nova (♩ = 126)
41

45
48
51
54
Gt. -Cornet 8' (Trumpet 8')
+Ch. to Gt.
Sw. -Krummhorn 8' (Oboe 8')

57
60
63
1
Gt. +Octave 4'
Ch. +Nazard 2⅔', Tierce 1⅗'
Ped. +4'
65
2

Ad page? -
Help